TINTORETTO

The life and work of the artist illustrated with 80 colour plates

ANNA PALLUCCHINI

THAMES AND HUDSON

Translated from the Italian by Pearl Sanders

Printed in Italy

ISBN 0 500 41042 9

Life

The term modernity, when applied to a painter of the past, can be misleading in present-day terms if it is taken to refer to an abstract and fragmented style of painting. But if we keep in mind what this sort of style is expressing – the attitude of its creator to reality and his own work – then Jacopo Tintoretto, the man who, according to Ridolfi, wished to be thought 'the most venturesome painter in the world', can be considered as our contemporary. Impelled by a tremendous creative fervour, he expressed his thoughts on vast canvases, in public and private buildings, in churches and guild halls, and, with the frescoes he painted on the outside of Venetian houses, helped to make the Venice of the time the most colourful, extrovert and welcoming of cities.

Titian should in a certain sense, be considered in the context of European art as a whole, because of the number of royal patrons for whom he worked and the friendships he made during his travels in Italy and Germany. Tintoretto, on the other hand, was a true Venetian, not only by birth, but because he lived his whole life in Venice, working mainly for the nobility and bourgeoisie of the city and extolling in various ways the two sources of strength which formed the basis for the power of the Republic: civic authority and an ardent faith in good works. The political history of the Republic was not always happy, and became less so once the city was drawn into the mainstream of events in sixteenth-century Italy and was forced to defend her colonies against the inexorable advance of the Turkish armies. Yet the religious life of Venice was one of extreme richness and intensity, reflecting the social consequences of the Protestant Reformation, anticipating the pressures of the Counter-Reformation, and transforming the economically motivated war against the infidel into a spiritual struggle. Jacopo Tintoretto spent his long and active creative life in this fervid atmosphere, in a society which was in the process of transformation, and under the vigilant eye of a government that knew how to harness all the collective and individual energies of the population to enrich the power and prestige of the community. Since he was not only an informed witness of the life of the Republic and the political, social and religious events of his time, but also an active participant, his art was not simply the expression of a complex and sensitive personality. It was also the expression of a particular, and extraordinarily dynamic, moment in history.

In the personal history of Jacopo Tintoretto there is, however, little to record. His exact date of birth is not definitely known; but from the document in the church of San Marziale, Venice, which records his death on 31 May 1594, and from other related factors, it is possible to deduce that he was born in 1518, the son of a citizen of Lucca, Giovanni Battista Robusti, a silk dyer (*tintore*). Nothing is known of his artistic training, except that it must have begun at a very early age if in 1539, when only twenty-one, he was already referred to as an independent master painter living in the parish of San Cassiano.

Early sources represent him as a self-taught genius who, after a very brief period of apprenticeship with Titian cut short by the jealousy of his great master, faced the difficulties of painting on his own, setting out to combine the form of Michelangelo with the colour of Titian. This ingenuous story, like all 'fables, contains an element of truth and has its own allegorical significance. What was meant by the 'form of Michelangelo', apart from a study of his drawings and casts known to have been in Venice at the time, was a whole culture of mannerism which had grown up in Venice through the influence of Paduan, Emilian, Tuscan and Roman artists working there and through the wide circulation of mannerist engravings. The 'colour of Titian' meant the culmination of that emphasis on colour, rooted in Byzantine mosaics, which belonged to the tradition of Venetian art and had been revitalized in the early years of the sixteenth century by the appearance of Giorgione and the flourishing school of artists that followed him. The allegorical significance of the legend lies in the view of Tintoretto as a precocious artist, who, as his friend

Calmo fully confirms, made enemies not only because of his great natural gifts, but also because of his exceptional enthusiasm and extraordinary capacity for work.

In fact what the critic Vuillemin calls Tintoretto's 'artistic orphanhood' is not to be taken at face value. It is reasonable to suppose that he was apprenticed at an early age to some little-known painter working in a tradition of solid craftsmanship; that he soon looked around and learned eagerly from the many Venetian artists who were already beginning to react against the influence of Giorgione; and that, at the same time, he constantly copied drawings, engravings and casts of antique and contemporary sculpture. More definitely, Ridolfi records the young artist as painting frescoes on the outside walls of Venetian houses and collaborating with Schiavone in painting small panels for furniture and wedding chests. Early art historians thought that *St Mark rescuing a slave* (*pls 19-21*) was the first of Tintoretto's important works to stir up the waters of Venetian painting, but we now know that it was the mature work of an artist who had been active as a master for almost ten years in an atmosphere which encouraged innovation. Moreover, late research has reconstructed a very interesting series of works which lead up to this painting and set it in its context. For this reason there now seems to be no need to postulate that Tintoretto must have travelled to Rome – a journey for which no tradition or documentary evidence exists. It is much more difficult to reject the possibility that, in about 1540, he may have gone to Mantua, that Mecca of post-Raphaelite mannerism dominated by Giulio Romano. Without postulating the influence of Giulio's bold inventions in perspective it would be difficult to explain the violent gestures and the treatment of the frame mouldings of the ceilings now in the Galleria Estense, Modena, executed by Tintoretto when he was little more than twenty.

By 1555 Tintoretto had already produced a considerable number of works for private individuals, churches and confraternities. In the same year he married Faustina Episcopi, the daughter of the superior of the Scuola di San Marco where the artist had begun to work on the decoration with a painting representing one of the saint's miracles. His wife was loving and devoted, according to contemporary testimony, and in their thirty years together eight children were born. At least three of them learned their father's craft and worked with him: Marietta (born 1556), Domenico (born 1560) and Marco (born 1561). Two other children, Perina and Altura, entered the convent of Santa Anna, and were so gifted at needlework that they were able to make an embroidered copy of the *Crucifixion* in the Scuola di San Rocco (the copy is now in the Kunsthistorisches Museum at Vienna). Ottavia (1570-1665), at the age of seventy, married a pupil of her brother Domenico named Sebastiano Casser, who inherited models and drawings belonging to the family and apparently made so bold as to sign his own paintings with the name of his great father-in-law. Marietta is known to have been a good painter and musician, and Domenico's artistic career was distinguished mainly in the field of portraiture; Marco, however, is better known for his lively character than for any artistic gifts.

To accommodate this large family, Tintoretto had moved to a large house in the parish of San Marziale. In 1574 he moved again to the Fondamento dei Mori, near the Madonna dell'Orto, the church for which he had already executed some important paintings, including the *Presentation of the Virgin* and the *Last Judgment*, and in which he was to be buried. He also owned a cottage on the mainland, at Carpenedo, where he could find scenery that was different from the water and clouds, architecture and skies which Venice offered, and where he could establish temporary contact with nature and indulge the taste for solitude mentioned by Ridolfi. Nevertheless he still found time to move in cultured circles and make friends such as Marcolini, a dilettante architect and a painter and engraver of fine books, Calmo, the talented playwright whose comedies satirized courtly manners, and Zarlino who was the choirmaster of St Mark's, as well as a composer and musical theorist. Music was, in fact, one of Tintoretto's interests, and Ridolfi records that he played the lute ' and other strange instruments of his own invention ', but, while musical gatherings and visits to the theatre (for which he designed scenery and costumes) may have provided relaxation from his feverish activity, they also helped his painting by giving concrete form to the ideas thrown up by his lively imagination.

The artist's life revolved around his work, as his enormous output shows, and it was not until he was approaching middle age, in about 1560, that he could count on the help of collaborators – young painters, many of them from Northern Europe like Marten de Vos, Pieter Vlerick (or Ulerich) and Paolo Franceschi, who came to his studio wishing to learn or perfect their art. In 1580 Tintoretto made his only recorded journey away from Venice, when he went with Faustina to Mantua to deliver a series of historical paintings commemorating exploits of the Gonzaga family. He was welcomed with honour by Duke Guglielmo Gonzaga, but returned after a few days, for, although he was now over sixty, the studio (where his children were also working) was extremely busy. Every work was drawn out and supervised by Tintoretto himself, whether it was a canvas for the Doge's Palace or a panel for an outlying parish like San Giuseppe di Castello, and the decorations for the Scuola di San Rocco were done almost entirely in his own hand.

There is no need to think of Tintoretto as a *peintre maudit* or subject his character to a psychoanalytic study to believe that he was a man devoured by a passion for painting. This passion was an end in itself and not a means of making money, for we know that he embarked on grandiose schemes of decoration for extremely modest rewards. Whereas Titian continually asked his royal patrons for money and benefits, Tintoretto gave his magnificent pictorial exposition of the Bible to the wealthy Confraternity of San Rocco for nothing. However, there was undoubtedly also an irrepressible need for understanding and recognition in the dyer's son, whose start in life had been far from easy, even if his *St Mark rescuing a slave* had aroused a good deal of controversy and discussion. It is in the light of these considerations that one must view his eagerness to obtain important commissions, such as the one for the Scuola di San Rocco (over which he was accused by other artists of ʻhitting below the belt') or for those in the Doge's Palace.

We are not fortunate enough to possess a catalogue of Tintoretto's library, as we do for El Greco, yet we can imagine that it must have been rather poor in works of the Hellenistic Greek period, and in the Renaissance literature which it inspired, and richer in the religious literature which was flourishing in Venice at the time, as it was in Spain and its European provinces. Indeed there can be no doubt of the artist's religious belief. In 1594, the year of his death, the man who had created a vast religious poem in the decorations of the Scuola di San Rocco painted for the last time the subject that was so dear to him: the *Last Supper*. In this work, painted for the Church of San Giorgio Maggiore, he filled the deep space with uneasy presences, with spirits and angels, in the manner of a man imagining what he will find at the frontier between life and death.

Works

Out of a vast production of over five hundred works attributed to Tintoretto by his contemporaries or by modern art historians, the dates of execution are known with certainty only for about twenty. Since the twenty include large schemes of decoration, ranging over a period between 1540 and 1594, it should be possible to draw up a chronological system into which the other paintings could be fitted, but this is not the case. Every chronological table which has been compiled represents a choice of position, so great are the differences which divide art historians. It is not easy to follow a clear-cut and constant line of development in the art of this painter, who has been aptly described by Newton as ʻerratic'. What can be said is that at the age of thirty he was already a mature artist and that he never denied his youth. While it is true to say that his early years in particular were marked by an extraordinary power of creation both in form and content, yet we cannot, with justice, regard the later pictures as irremediably weakened by his great technical facility – we need think only of the San Rocco and San Giorgio Maggiore canvases to be convinced of this. Of course, there are signs of fatigue in certain passages of this huge output, especially when Tintoretto was not able to use his art to express his inner life (Ridolfi spoke of the artist's 'need to unburden a mind filled with countless thoughts'). When this happened, instead of a deeply loved and honoured profession, his art became a service, and he found himself constrained by the demands of patrons to paint commemorative works for which he felt no sympathy – this is especially apparent in the canvases painted for the Doge's Palace. But if certain stylistic traits have been borrowed from his art and cheapened by the excessive repetition of later imitators, it is not Tintoretto's fault. There is only one artist who, even though their methods differed, can be regarded as his worthy spiritual successor: Domenikos Theotokopoulos, known as El Greco.

We have mentioned the impossibility of assigning any particular master to Tintoretto. According to the custom of the time he would certainly have been apprenticed in an artist's studio in about 1530, when he was twelve years old, and we know that, by the age of twenty, he was already an independent master; therefore his artistic education must have occurred during the ten years 1530-40. The early works reveal that he had a remarkable capacity for assimilating the styles of Titian and other leading Venetian painters: the thick impasto of Bonifazio de' Pitati was adapted to the elegant forms of Paris Bordone, the easy, flowing narrative style of Schiavone was extended to encompass Pordenone's innovations in perspective and his massive sculptural manner. I believe that Pordenone's frescoes in the cloister of Santo Stefano (1532) had an important influence on Tintoretto, even though this influence is not noticeable before 1540.

These Venetian artists belonged to a generation influenced and rejuvenated by the stylistic developments then taking place in Central Italy – developments foreshadowed by

Raphael, Michelangelo, and their followers. Moreover, in 1527 Aretino and Jacopo Sansovino arrived in Venice, bringing from Florence and Rome pictorial ideas and forms which were to have a considerable influence on the painting of the northern city. In 1535 Aretino received from Vasari drawings of the Medici tombs (Ridolfi states that Tintoretto imitated them in one of his early works, a fresco on the Palazzo Gussoni at Santa Fosca); in 1537 Sansovino began the bas-reliefs for St Mark's; and, as Longhi has pointed out, some of the formal, typological and dramatic elements in these sculptures were later used by Tintoretto.

The network of manneristic elements which has been examined in detail by L. Coletti and R. Pallucchini as a source of inspiration for Venetian painting after Giorgione was made up of two factors: the presence in Venice of artists who were imbued with that culture, and the import of engravings. Through the medium of engravings the works of artists from other parts of Italy were made known: Raphael, engraved by Raimondi; Michelangelo, by Vico and Ghisi; the Emilian school, by Caraglio Bonasone, Ugo da Carpi and Antonio da Trento; Giulio Romano, by Agostino Veneziano. An important centre in this connection must have been the printing-house of Marcolini, who, in a letter to Aretino of 1551, referred to Tintoretto as 'like my son', and who, as early as 1540, had published *Le Ingegnose Sorti* with illustrations by Giuseppe Salviati. Salviati worked in Venice and its surroundings for many years, producing numerous drawings of biblical scenes as well as the mosaics for St Mark's fountain, and was certainly an important influence on Tintoretto's early years – although at a later stage the Venetian tradition in turn affected and transformed the style of the Tuscan artist. Arcangeli has rightly said that Tintoretto came 'at the heart of the great manneristic process, after Parmigianino, Primaticcio, Camillo Boccaccino, alongside Schiavone, Salviati ... before Tibaldi and Veronese', for, in the same year that Tintoretto painted *St Mark rescuing a slave* (*pls 19-21*), Veronese was painting the *Bevilacqua Lazise altarpiece*, a work still provincial in style.

In the light of present-day scholarship, the first work

ascribed to Tintoretto is the votive painting *Marcello* in a private collection in Lucerne, dating from about 1537 and formerly ascribed to Pordenone. There is also the outstanding *Madonna and Child with Saints*, in the Leger Collection, which is dated 1540 and carries a mysterious monogram, but is a firm link in the chain reconstructed by Pallucchini. The most remarkable of the interesting series of stylistically related Madonnas is, without doubt, the one in the Palazzo Curtiss in Venice; it is an elegant and stylistically advanced painting, especially noteworthy as an early example of the creation of depth in space, which was to become one of the most important elements in Tintoretto's art. Also dating from around 1540 are the ceiling panels depicting mythological scenes in the Galleria Estense, Modena; these, too, create a feeling of depth, with the forms moving freely about in space. They were probably painted for the Palazzo Pisani at San Paterniano, and the interesting thing is that they were executed *before* Titian's Santo Spirito ceilings, which, together with his *Battle of Cadore* and *Ecce Homo* in Vienna, are probably the most illusionistic and manneristic of that artist's works. We have already referred to the influence of Mantuan art on the interesting Modena paintings, which are unfortunately in a very poor condition. Because the feeling for space which distinguishes these works is not present, the curious *Disputation* in Milan is to be dated somewhat earlier; it is, as Arcangeli wrote, a ' disputation which may have some reference to matters concerning art '.

It was in the period 1540-5 that Tintoretto was closest to Andrea Schiavone, and may have collaborated with him. Schiavone was six years older, not yet subject to the influence of Parmigianino, which was later to debilitate his work, and still able to tackle fresco painting (Palazzo Zen ai Gesuiti, which Ridolfi says was painted in collaboration with the young Tintoretto). The decoration of marriage chests, which early writers say was a typical activity of Schiavone, was also undertaken by Tintoretto with lively imagination: the biblical scenes in Vienna (*pls 2-7*) are examples. The sense of movement in the architectural structure and figure groupings, and the attractive colour and play of light and shade, reveal the capacity for narrative art which the artist had developed, following the examples of Bonifazio, Schiavone and the biblical engravings of Giuseppe Salviati.

There is some doubt as to whether the ceiling to which Aretino refers in his letters of 1545 is the same as the *Apollo and Marsyas*, in the Hartford collection (*pl. 1*). However, the peaceful encounter of noble beings, the perfect oval of the composition, and the absence of those foreshortenings recommended by Paolo Pino in his *Dialogo di pittura* (1548), were probably intended to please the taste of the patron as well as the artist. Nevertheless Aretino must later have come to appreciate the young painter's stylistic innovations, for he was moved to defend *St Mark rescuing a slave* (*pls 19-21*) in words which would have displeased his friend Titian. But before we discuss that famous work, to which recent cleaning has restored its original splendour of colour, we must not overlook the pair of paintings executed for the presbytery of San Marcuola: the *Last Supper* (*pls 10-12*), dated 1547 and still *in situ*, and *Christ washing the feet of his disciples* (*pls 15-18*), which was soon taken to Spain. If it were not obvious that these are pendants, it would be difficult to imagine that two such dissimilar works could have been painted at the same time: the almost archaic frontal treatment of the *Last Supper* and its constricted space, compare strangely with the irregular arrangement of the groups under the majestic porch in *Christ washing the feet of his disciples*. What the two paintings have in common are the characters, who are ordinary men and women, and their lifelike gestures and actions which are conveyed not by a diligent study of mimicry, but by rapid strokes of light.

Apart from the early portraits (*Portrait of a nobleman*, dated 1545, at Hampton Court, *Portrait of a man aged 39*, in the Uffizi, *Self-portraits* in London and Boston), the paintings executed by Tintoretto in the same period as the San Marcuola paintings (*Esther and Ahasuerus*, in the Escurial, *Christ washing the feet of his disciples*, in the Lord Pembroke collection, *The Woman Taken in Adultery*, in Dresden) form a close-knit group which foreshadows *St*

Mark rescuing a slave of 1548. Aretino praised this last work for the 'naturalness' of its foreshortening, and Calmo for its 'fine conception in the presentation of gestures, manners, majesty, foreshortenings, profiles, shadows and distances and perspectives'. Another brilliant example of Tintoretto's narrative gift dates from the following year: *St Roch visiting sufferers from the plague*, in the Church of San Rocco. This is a picture of a hospital, and the gloomy, unbreatheable atmosphere is brilliantly conveyed in a way which caused a sensation at the time.

In 1550-1 Tintoretto painted a series of pictures illustrating stories from the Book of Genesis for the Scuola della Trinità. The four which survive, *The Creation of the Animals* (*pls 29-30*), *The Fall of Man* (*pls 31-2*) and *Cain and Abel*, all in the Accademia, Venice, and *Adam and Eve at the Tree of Knowledge* in the Uffizi, show a more marked influence of Titian in the attempt to imprison light in colour and to create volume through the use of a graduated chiaroscuro. These paintings also reveal a rare feeling for landscape which leads on to the masterpiece *Susanna and the elders* (*pls 42-4*) – a marvellous harmony of line, colour and light.

The spring-like atmosphere and the transparent light on the body of Susanna were not achieved by chance. Between 1553 and 1555 we can point to works which were plainly inspired by a study of Veronese. This can be seen especially in the emphasis on colour, the adoption of bold effects of perspective, and the decorative style of the links between figure and figure in such works as the *Crucifixion* in San Severo, the *Assumption of the Virgin* in the Gesuiti, the *Circumcision* in the Accademia, the six *Biblical Legends* in the Prado and *St Ursula and her Virgins* (*pl. 37*). This influence extended through the whole of this group of works, from the distortion of the figure of the Virgin in the *Assumption,* a candid declaration of Tintoretto's admiration, to the very personal assimilation of Veronese's art into his own private idiom in the Prado paintings or the procession of the Virgins in *St Ursula*. At the same time the organ doors in the Church of Madonna dell'Orto (*pl. 35*), which are documented to between 1551 and 1556, with their simple

13

forms, polished execution and predominance of light over shadow, echo that revelation of a serene universe brought to Venice by the young Caliari, who was active in the Doge's Palace in 1553.

The lightening of his colour and the use of more subtle tones enabled Tintoretto to construct large compositions without relying solely on perspective, peopling space with numerous figures and evanescent crowds, as in *Moses bringing forth water from the rock* (*pls 38-9*) or *The Miracle of the Loaves and Fishes* in the Metropolitan Museum, New York. After the brilliant treatment of the organ loft in the Church of Santa Maria del Giglio (1557), where the evangelists appear to be thrust on to ominous clouds by the force of the artist's brush (*pls 45-6*), Tintoretto continued his search for a way of rendering light with *The Miracle of the Paralytic* (*pls 67-9*). This painting was to be placed opposite one by Pordenone, a fact which must have encouraged Tintoretto to accentuate the formal tension, based on the interplay of curved lines forming links between the figures. The same psychological weight is also a feature of two other canvases painted at about the same time: *Aeneas bidding farewell to Dido*, in Brunswick, and the romantic *Rescue of Arsinoë*, in Dresden.

Probably to be dated 1561 are two other remarkable compositions, where the tension is relaxed and the emphasis is on luminous colour: *The Discovery of the True Cross* (*pls 52-3*), where the elegant figures are almost all lit from below, and *The Marriage at Cana* in the sacristy of Santa Maria della Salute, where all the elements in the composition are brought together in perfect harmony to create a sense of depth in space – geometric perspective and gradation of colour and, especially, of light. This mastery of form, colour and light enabled Tintoretto to paint that enchanting landscape *St George slaying the Dragon* (*pls 25-6*), where, as Newton says, the sky and city of towers have the suggestive power of a painting by Altdorfer.

In 1562, after a gap of more than twenty years, Tintoretto returned to the subject of the legend of St Mark. He was commissioned by the great physician, Tommaso Rangone, to do a cycle of paintings for presentation to the Scuola Grande di San Marco. Rangone, a friend of the painter Jacopo Sansovino (who appears to have suggested some of the themes and details in the compositions), appears as the donor in all three canvases. They are: *The Finding of St Mark's Body (pl. 55)*, the finest of the three, with the vault illuminated by torchlight and by the mysterious glow which accompanies the appearance of the saint; *The Removal of St Mark's Body (pl. 54)*, where a storm extinguishes the funeral pyre and devastates the public square in Alexandria — a square vaguely reminiscent of St Mark's in Venice; and finally *St Mark Rescuing the Saracen*, the most damaged of the three canvases, but one which must have possessed a remarkable power of suggestion and richness of fantasy, to judge by the praise of contemporary writers.

Tintoretto's *tour de force* of this period was two paintings in the apse of the church of the Madonna dell'Orto. They are of extraordinary height, and the artist goes beyond the formal and psychological tensions of the individual pictures to dwell on the contrast between the two scenes. *The Adoration of the Golden Calf*, while enjoyable in certain details, is an elaborate and somewhat pretentious historical tableau of the kind known in France as a *grande machine*; it is a static composition, with quite distinct superimposed areas, such as are found in ancient Byzantine mosaics. *The Last Judgment (pl. 56)*, on the other hand, is a complex composition built on a spiral, in which the numerous figures are brought together by means of a unifying light. It is an astonishing work even if not an intensely moving one; and it even captivated the hard-to-please Vasari, who complained only of a lack of 'finish' (far from necessary, in my opinion).

If a comparison with its great precursor, *The Last Judgment* of Michelangelo, is inevitable, this merely serves to underline the differences between the two conceptions. Michelangelo represents the tragic particles of humanity falling through a compressed and abstracted space; while Tintoretto's unrestrained imagination creates a multiple spatiality, which draws the spectator into it like a vortex. There was also a fundamental difference between their religious beliefs: for Tintoretto, faith was a consolation and support in his life and work; for Michelangelo it was a dramatic realization of the condition of man and the artist. It must also be understood that Tintoretto's knowledge of the work of Michelangelo was based on very fragmentary sources, casts, drawings and engravings, and he took from it only certain details, such as the sinuous figures and a sense of the power of the restrained movement, the half-finished gesture. Certain particular drawings of Michelangelo, such as *The Risen Christ* (to be found in a letter dated 1535) became prototypes for Tintoretto's drawings, but they are always studies of individual figures in movement, images caught in a flash; there exist only two Tintoretto drawings of complete compositions, one in Berlin for the Munich *Venus, Vulcan and Mars*, the other in Naples for the Munich *Battle on the Taro*.

How was it possible for Tintoretto to build up large compositions from these fragments, from formal situations copied from life, but still more from statuary, from the engravings of Italian mannerists and northern artists, from Dürer to Lucas van Leyden? No sketches exist; but *modelli* prepared for competitions, such as the one for *Paradise* in the Doge's Palace, are another matter; it seems that Tintoretto put his ideas straight onto canvas, painting with rapid brushstrokes, and then worked over the details with the help of his drawings, some of which he used again and again for years. According to contemporary eyewitnesses, he solved problems of lighting by making model theatres with small figures which were illuminated as need arose, just as they would be on a stage: an obvious example occurs in the small painting, the *Parable of the Wise and Foolish Virgins* in the Boymans van Beuningen Museum, Rotterdam.

Tintoretto devoted a large part of his activity between 1564 and 1587 to the San Rocco paintings which are much more successful than those in the Madonna dell'Orto. These canvases are the result of an exceptionally happy relationship between artist and patron. The patron in this case was the Confraternity of San Rocco, whose magnificent headquarters had been completed about the year 1560. It had grown rich mainly through the large quantities of charitable gifts which flowed in as a result of the public devotion to St Roch or Rock (1295-1327), protector against the plague which was a recurring scourge in sixteenth-century Venice, as in other parts of Italy. The original function of the lay brotherhood was to render assistance in times of epidemic, but it soon enlarged its scope and became a charitable organization in a wider sense. Together with other important brotherhoods it participated in a vast philanthropic enterprise, which acquired considerable social and political importance since it helped to some extent to redistribute wealth and so prevented some of the social disturbances caused by poverty and hardship. In order to understand the subject of Tintoretto's paintings – the salvation of the body and spirit – it is essential to bear in mind that they were painted for the Confraternity and thus for the poor of Venice who came there for alms. It has been said that the special relationship which developed between Tintoretto and his patrons led to a certain degree of freedom for the artist, but this is only partly true. In fact all the stages of his work were very closely followed by the directors of the Confraternity; and, among the conservative nobility, there was unfavourable criticism of the innovations he introduced, which some people found disturbing and offensive. There is no doubt, however, that the relationship between Tintoretto and the directors of the Scuola di San Rocco was particularly fortunate, for he was an artist whose spiritual faith made him especially well suited to record the religious life of Venice which had gained new strength through the ferments and upheavals of the Catholic Reformation.

The premises of the Confraternity had been completed in 1545, but it was not until 1564 that it was decided to commission decorations for the interior. Tintoretto realized how congenial such a theme would be to him, and tried by all means in his power to obtain the commission. Vasari wove quite a romance around the story: starting with the idea of a competition for the first ceiling arranged in 1564 (and historically verified), he went on to describe Tintoretto's stratagem of producing for it not a drawing but the finished *Glory of St Roch* already *in situ*, so asserting his superiority over the other indignant competitors, Giuseppe Salviati, Paolo Veronese and Federico Zuccaro.

He set to work so eagerly that by the end of 1565 he had completed the enormous *Crucifixion* (*pls 57-59*). This work marks an important stage in the development of Tintoretto's style, and can be said to conclude the period of the early works and initiate a new phase. Its most important stylistic elements are the circumscribed space, the centrality of the composition, the calculated arrangement of the groups, and the epic tone of the tragedy which is depicted in a classical manner without any eloquent or uncontrolled gestures, the force of the emotion being conveyed largely by the livid effects of light. A similar controlled pathos characterizes the other canvases in the Sala dell'Albergo (*pls 60-64*) which were completed in 1567. Almost ten years were to pass before Tintoretto returned to San Rocco to resume his activity, this time in the upper hall. (Nevertheless the San Rocco paintings seem to have represented a personal obligation for him, as if he desired to create a gigantic and personal *ex-voto* with his own hand – a letter he wrote to the heads of the Society in 1577 explains that ' I wish to show the great love I bear this our revered School, because of my devotion to its glorious master St Roch '.

However, other works executed at the same time reveal the participation of the artists of his studio, which was now flourishing: the paintings for San Cassiano, the lost *Last Judgment* painted for the Doge's Palace, and the paintings in the Church of San Rocco. Outstanding among the works of this decade for their bold composition and their special artistic merit are *St Roch in Prison*, which marks a new development in Tintoretto's study of light, and *The Last Supper* in the church of San Polo which was painted just after 1570. Whereas in *The Last Supper* in the church of San Trovaso (*pls 48-50*), painted about 1560, there is still a contained rhythm which accords with the feeling of stupefaction experienced by the apostles at the news of the betrayal of Christ, in the San Polo version the action is dramatized by the dynamic treatment of space and arrangement of figures, setting the seal upon the rite of the institution of the Eucharist. Also, by including the poor receiving the gift of bread, Tintoretto is already hinting at the connection between faith and good works which was to be developed at San Rocco. A tendency to elongate the figures in a manneristic style is to be found again in the contemporary paintings for the Libreria, five *Philosophers* (see *pl. 65*). It was almost certainly due to Titian that, in 1557, Tintoretto was excluded from the decoration of the great hall (on which such uncontroversial painters as Paolo Veronese, Gian Battista Zelotti, Giuseppe Salviati and Giovanni Battista Franco were employed). Tintoretto was content to contribute his noble figures of philosophers, conceived as inspired biblical prophets, only a few of which remain in existence.

In 1576 Tintoretto began the second series of paintings for the upper hall of the Scuola di San Rocco. At the beginning of July 1575 he had offered to paint the central canvas for the ceiling; in August 1576, at the Festival of St Roch, this canvas, The *Adoration of the Brazen Serpent*, was in its place. Tintoretto then offered to supply three paintings for the Festival every year, leaving it to the directors to fix the amount of his fee but asking for an annuity of 100 ducats to compensate him in case of illness. This offer was accepted and a commission of three members was established to approve the paintings. It is symptomatic that, only a few years after the closure of the Council of Trent (1563) and the publication of Giglio's book on the 'abuses of painters', the Confraternity wished to exercise control over the artist's work; but, in spite of this, he was able to compose his epic with an extraordinary degree of freedom, ignoring the dictates of the Counter-Reformation concerning iconography and instead going direct to the sources of the religious texts in order to stress the comforting theme of salvation from the physical and moral ills to which humanity is subject. Three large ceiling paintings: The *Brazen Serpent*, The *Gathering of the Manna* and *Moses bringing forth water from the rock*, portray Old Testament instances of liberation from bodily ills, sickness, hunger and thirst; while the canvases on the walls, which narrate the life of Christ, celebrate victory over spiritual ills through the institution of Baptism (water) and Communion (bread), and the certainty of victory over worldly inducements (the Temptation) and over death (the Resurrection). The conjunction of the two groups forms a concordance of Old and New Testament cases of divine intervention to alleviate suffering along the lines of the illustrated *biblia pauperum* in use at the time. Other smaller panels on the walls and ceiling are *The Sacrifice of Isaac, The Salvation of Jonah, Elijah receiving food from the Angel, Elisha multiplying the loaves*, etc. In the two large end paintings the tumultuous scenes, with surging crowds of agitated bystanders and the searing light which strongly models the foreshortened figures, contrast with the central picture, *The Gathering of the Manna*, with its glowing light and calm, pastoral rhythm. In the small panels, the figures are only with difficulty contained within the framework and are agitated by violent movements, accentuated by sudden bursts of light. The oval representing the angel restraining the arm of Isaac is particularly beautiful, and the oblique angle of vision in the group of Jonah and the whale is most skilful, the whole scene being illuminated by the dazzling apparition of God. The tension in the composition of the *Temptation of Adam* suggests a rotary motion, while the corresponding oval depicting the *Paschal Feast* is extremely original in conception: the solemn, absorbed figures are moulded by the light of the fire on which lie the remains of the lamb.

On the walls are alternating scenes which differ in their treatment of space and light according to their subjects: the festive *Nativity* (*pls 70-73*), the dramatic *Baptism of Christ* (*pls 74-75*), the violent impetus of the *Resurrection*, the receding space in the background to the *Last Supper*. One of the finest of these paintings is the visionary *Ascension*, where Christ is surrounded by adoring angels; on the bottom left of the painting, one of the apostles, whose function is that of the chorus in a mystery play, bends as if swept down by the impetus of the triumphant Christ who 'passes through air and fire, penetrates all material heavens'. The quotation is taken from a text by Mattia Bellintani, a contemporary preacher whose imagination portrayed events in a way which came very close to the iconography adopted by Tintoretto, emphasizing the dramatic and dynamic elements. In the *Baptism of Christ* (*pls 74-75*) and the *Flight into Egypt* (*pls 85-86*), in particular, the similarity is so great that it is difficult to believe it could have been accidental.

We do not know the order in which Tintoretto painted the San Rocco canvases; we know that the decoration of the upper hall was completed in 1581 and that work on the lower hall took place in 1583-7. In these great canvases, all the artist's skill, as well as his unceasing experimentation with the problems of form and light, were employed in a Biblical exegesis, in which reality and unreality, the natural and the supernatural, combine to form an inseparable unity. It seems almost impossible to imagine that at nearly the same time, in 1577, he could also have painted the allegorical works for the Sala dell'Anticollegio in the Doge's Palace. In these elegant fables, the mythological characters move in intricate arabesques, and light, which in the San Rocco paintings was used to create dramatic contrasts, here serves to construct – indeed, almost to caress – the forms; colour, too, which served an expressive function in the San Rocco paintings, creating tensions of chiaroscuro, is here a means for producing subtle effects and half-tones. The relaxation of tension does, however, result in a somewhat academic manner. These few paintings marked the beginning of a new period of intense activity in the decoration of the Doge's Palace. With considerable assistance from his studio, Tintoretto painted many votive and commemorative works in the years 1578-88, culminating in *Paradise,* for the Great Council Chamber. Perhaps the finest of the paintings commemorating the victories of the Republic is *The Battle of Zara*, in the Sala dello Scrutinio, masterly in its treatment of masses and light (see pp. 24-5). In the seventeenth century the public taste for battle scenes led to the development of this type of painting into a real pictorial *genre* where the artist could display his skill in staging complex crowd movements; as early as 1578,

Tintoretto had already procured a commission for a commemorative series depicting the glorious deeds of the Gonzaga family. This cycle of eight canvases, now in Munich, certainly owes much to assistants, but it is obvious that the composition of the battle scenes is by the hand of Tintoretto himself. He plays on the contrast between the modelled groups in the foreground and the small evanescent figures in the backgrounds, and animates the arabesques of struggling bodies at the front by his skilful arrangement of light upon the swarming crowds at the back.

Even after the age of sixty Tintoretto was able to do great things in his own hand, as we can see when we look at the lower hall of the Scuola di San Rocco. The Life of Christ was again the theme, but this time with greater emphasis on the cult of the Virgin. Because the hall was rather dark, Tintoretto accentuated his existing practice of giving less importance to colour and decreasing its tension in order to concentrate on the powerful effect created by the composition itself. Light was given the task of revealing the plastic consistency of objects. This consistency could become more and more fragile, dematerialized to the farthest limit; that limit was not to be surpassed until the following century, by Rembrandt.

In the lower hall of San Rocco an iconography combining various tendencies was employed in the vast paintings: the *Annunciation* portrays the Virgin in her humble home, startled by the joyous entry of the angels, while, as Ruskin says, the sound of the plane and hammer of St Joseph can be heard in the background. If we compare this painting with the traditional *Annunciation* in the neighbouring church of San Rocco, this seems a very romantic version. The *Adoration of the Magi* plays upon the contrasts between foreground and background that Tintoretto had often employed successfully in the Gonzaga paintings. The *Flight into Egypt (pls 85-6)* is seen as a fable set in an extraordinary landscape. The *Massacre of the Innocents* poses problems of attribution which are still being debated by historians. The two small terminal canvases, depicting hermits in a landscape, undoubtedly mark an extraordinary stage in the evolution of the artist's style, as well as of his spiritual development and that of his time.

In this period Tintoretto, with the assistance of his studio, painted other votive works for the Doge's Palace and *The Life of St Catherine* cycle for the Church of Santa Caterina (now in the Accademia) in which the scene of the *Martyrdom* is outstanding for its tormented spatiality. His last message is that of a visionary: in the *Battle between St Michael and Satan*, in Dresden, he recalled his memories of Dürer's engravings, with an effect which was almost medieval. He showed this visionary power again in his cosmic vision of *Paradise*, for which a wonderful small sketch exists in the Louvre (*pls 83-4*), and in *The Last Supper*, in the Church of San Giorgio (*pls 87-90*), painted in 1594, the year of his death.

To complete this rapid survey of the artist's activity, we must consider his portraiture. Most critics agree that in this field he could not compete either with the majestic figures of Titian or the intimate art of Lotto. The chronological sequence of portraits known to be by Tintoretto follows the same stylistic evolution as his other paintings: at first he was influenced by the elegant forms of Salviati and the warm, enveloping atmosphere beloved by Titian, but later he tended more and more in the direction of psychological insight and immediacy. His portraiture was not confined to formal pictures, where the sitter was the subject of the composition, but appeared in many of his other works as well, where portraits of living people were included in the crowd scenes, often in the most unlikely moments and places – at the foot of the Cross, or in the dark abyss of limbo. It may in fact be that his ability to render the movement and psychology of crowds turned Tintoretto away from the search for a new approach to individual portraiture; moreover, numerous commissions for group portraits of members of Confraternities and patrons, for the most part modest and unobtrusive people, led him to seek a close physical likeness rather than stress the individual character of the sitter, so that he consciously sacrificed the concept of the individual to the portrayal of his rank and social positon. However, with the passage of time, as his own spiritual insight matured, he succeeded in penetrating more deeply into the character of the individual. In the portraits of old men, especially, he managed to convey the sense of the fragility of the physical shell which was kept alive by a tenacious inner force. This was how Tintoretto must have appeared to his contemporaries, if we are to believe the description of Calmo and the self-portraits in London and Boston: his inner strength was nourished by his belief in the creative power of the artist and the sincere faith in prayer and good works which he shared with the common people.

Studies of archers for 'The Battle of Zara' *(see p. 21).* *Florence, Uffizi*

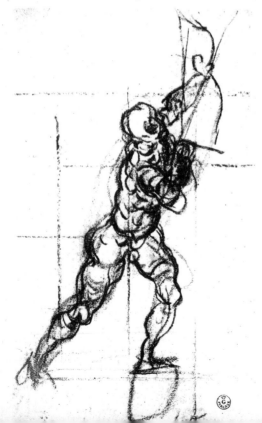

Tintoretto and the Critics

Ever since his own time, Tintoretto's forceful character has aroused both praise and criticism. We have already mentioned Aretino, at first an admirer of the painter's innovations, but later unable to appreciate his rapid manner of working. We find a similar critical attitude in Francesco Sansovino in 1556 and in Vasari in 1568. If the admiration of Ridolfi (1648) cannot be entirely justified from a critical standpoint, Marco Boschini (1660) grasped the subtleties of the artist's treatment of light, and his follower, Roger de Pyles (1699), goes further into this aspect, showing the connection between light and the beginnings of movement, which arises not so much from the dynamics of the figures as from '*grandes glissades de lumière et d'ombre*'.

Neither the academicism of the eighteenth century nor the romanticism of the nineteenth was able fully to come to terms with Tintoretto, although his greatness continued to be recognized. Ruskin praised his power of suggestion.

Criticism in the present century begins with a monograph by Thode (1901) who saw the artist's style as exemplifying the use of light to master the contrast between form and colour and so achieve a spiritualization of reality. German art historians have undertaken a reconstruction of the chronology and stylistic development of Tintoretto's painting, following the line of criticism suggested by contemporary Expressionist art (von Hadeln, von der Berken, Mayer Tietze). The school of criticism which views the artist as an expression of his environment has its exponents in Dvořák (1918-21), who first considered the relationship between Tintoretto and the world of mannerism; Vipper (1951), who discussed the links between his art and the social and spiritual climate of Venice during the second half of the sixteenth century; and Sartre (1957), who followed the same line of thought, but carried it to extreme conclusions. The most important reappraisals of Tintoretto's art have been made by Italian critics, notably Pittaluga (1952) and Coletti (1944). The reconstruction of the artist's early years by Rodolfo Pallucchini (1950) is a fundamental contribution, while Eric Newton (1952), a passionate admirer of Tintoretto, has written a work veined by a Ruskinian sensibility, but brought up to date from a scientific point of view, concluding with a defence of the substantial limitations suggested by Longhi. The reader should also refer to the excellent article on Tintoretto by Rodolfo Pallucchini in the *Encyclopaedia of World Art* (McGraw Hill, 1967) where an extensive bibliography will also be found.

Notes on the Plates

1 Apollo and Marsyas, c. 1545. Oil on canvas, 137×236 cm. Hartford, Conn., Wadsworth Atheneum. The letter from Aretino thanking Tintoretto for two ceiling paintings, *Apollo and Marsyas* and *Argus and Mercury*, was dated 1545. Historians agree that the former is this present canvas, which has a decorative rhythm, clear colour tones and a flowing style reminiscent of Schiavone. Some of the expressions employed by Aretino to refer to the figures ('beautiful and alert and living') and a consideration of some of the much live'ier works which preceded this painting have caused Arcangeli (1955) to wonder whether this might perhaps be an earlier work. However, it must be remembered that Tintoretto had to take account of the special taste of Aretino.

2-3 The Feast of Belshazzar, c. 1545. Oil on panel, 29×157 cm. Vienna, Kunsthistorisches Museum. Painted at the time which has been described (Pallucchini, 1950) as the period when Tintoretto's art was closest to that of Schiavone. We no longer possess the frescoes on which, according to early sources, the two artists collaborated, but we do still have a fine series of marriage chests (*cassoni*). Here the narrative e'ement derived from Bonifazio acquires a greater freedom and complexity through the use of the rapid technique of Schiavone – 'faster than an arrow shot by Saracen hand', according to Boschini. This painting is tasteful in its details and description of costumes, and striking in the complexity of its spatial construction, with groups of figures creating a succession of centres of interest, giving no rest to the viewer.

4-6 The Prostration of Bathsheba, c. 1545. Oil on panel, 29×155 cm. Vienna, Kunsthistorisches Museum. For historical information see note to previous plate. The freedom and rich imagination of Tintoretto's composition is apparent also in this panel from a marriage chest, where the foreground pattern of figures linked in a circular sweep is repeated in the background, creating a perfect spatial unity. The fantastic architecture serves to comment upon and integrate the structural function of the figures.

5-7 The Promise to David, c. 1545. Oil on panel, 29×155 cm. Vienna, Kunsthistorisches Museum. For historical information see note to *pls 2-3*. While the general arrangement is dictated by the shape of the panel, details examined in isolation foreshadow devices used in the artist's later and larger works: in this case the floating figure on the right is particularly noticeable. The ability to suggest space and the swooping curves which link the figures also presage the power and unity of pictures such as the *Crucifixion* in the Scuola di San Rocco.

8-9 Concert of Women, c. 1545. Oil on canvas, 49×90 cm. Verona, Museo Civico. Although some critics are doubtful, Berenson's attribution of this work to Tintoretto is accepted by most. It is a very early painting, dating from the period when Tintoretto was using a particularly decorative and refined manner inspired by Schiavone. It was painted later than the Vienna marriage chests.

10-12 Last Supper, 1547. Oil on canvas, 157×443 cm. Venice, San Marcuo'a. Completed on 27 August 1547, as shown by the inscription. This *Last Supper* is treated in a traditional manner, laid out across the picture plane, and shows no striving for effects, although there is an urgency and tension in the conversation of the apostles. There is an amazing ambiguity in the two figures on the sides, recognized as allegories of Faith and Charity, but so well incorporated into the action that they could be taken for two humble servants at the poor inn, if it were not for the mysterious aura which surrounds them.

13-14 The Woman taken in Adultery, c. 1547. Oil on canvas, 119×169 cm.·Rome, Gal'eria Nazionale. This is a fairly early work, still showing the influence of Schiavone in the typology of the characters, the elongation of the figures, the clear and flowing colour; but a new and mature element which now appears, as in the similar version of the same subject in Amsterdam, is the vast sweep of the perspective which closely resembles *Christ washing the feet of his disciples* (see the next note).

15-18 Christ washing the feet of his disciples, 1547. Oil on canvas, 160×440 cm. Madrid, Prado. Dated. Originally the pendant to *The Last Supper* in San Marcuola (see above), from which it differs in setting out to construct a vast and complex internal space. This is achieved not so much by the use of architectural elements as by the arrangement of isolated groups of figures, which convey no sense of movement or animation. Although there is no affectation in the treatment of the individual figures, they are all examples of brilliant draughtsmanship and naturalistic observation: note the apostle unlacing his shoes, or the one taking the stocking from his companion. The light entering from the right illuminates the interior and emphasizes the shapes of objects; beyond the portico, a blinding light falls upon the clear-cut architectural forms, which are taken from a treatise on architecture by Sebastiano Serlio.

19-21 St Mark rescuing a slave, 1548. Oil on canvas, 415×544 cm. Venice, Accademia. Completed in April 1548, according to a letter from Aretino which praised the painting but sounded a note of reservation about the 'swiftness' of the brushstroke. Recent cleaning (in 1966) has revealed a freshness of colour and atmospheric background which is less close to Titian than had always been believed, and is well adapted to the dynamics of this very manneristic type of composition. There is perhaps an over-abundance of themes: the crowd, and the portraits of living people which make it up; the skilful arrangement of groups and individuals; the rich colour and the light which orders the composition of space. This is the mature result of the knowledge gained during ten years of tireless experimentation.

22-23 St Augustine healing forty cripples, 1549-50. Oil on canvas, 170×255 cm. Vicenza, Museo Civico. Detail. Painted for the altar of the Godi family in the church of San Michele, Vicenza. This work can be dated on the basis of its similarity to *St Roch visiting sufferers from the plague* in the church of San Rocco, Venice. Pallucchini points out that the power of this manneristic work lies in the element of fantasy created by Tintoretto's particular treatment of light. The composition, in which two side wings enclose a space where the tormented figures of the lame appear, recalls that of the *Baptism* by Jacopino del Conte (1541); but this is only a superficial resemblance suggested by a similar formal approach.

24 Portrait of Jacopo Soranzo, c. 1550. Oil on canvas, 75×60 cm. Milan, Castello Sforzesco. This work formed the centrepiece of a group of portraits depicting fifteen members of the Soranzo family. The other portraits are still in existence, but in a very bad state, and are to be seen in the same museum. The portrait of Jacopo is of the head and shoulders only, whereas the other members of the family are portrayed almost full length, seated in a hierarchic order. From calculations of the ages of the sitters, it seems that Jacopo was over eighty; but the strength of character which can be seen behind his worn features confirms him as still the authoritative head of the family. It is as if an inner light, rather than the glimmer in the dark room, illuminated his hollowed face, the beard and the white hair.

25-26 St George slaying the dragon, c. 1550. Oil on canvas, 157×99 cm. London, National Gallery. Probably painted at the time when Tintoretto's interest in landscape was at its height. The composition is built on a stratification of planes, defined by an interplay of curves. The terrain rises towards the green wood and the green walls of the dream-like city. From the sea to the forest, these variations on a single colour, varying in luminosity, form a background to the kneeling figure of the princess, her silk cloak undulating behind her, her face almost impassive in spite of her fear. The background of sky and city walls is transfigured with a sensibility worthy of an Altdorfer.

27-28 Venus, Vulcan and Mars, c. 1551. Oil on canvas, 134×198 cm. Munich, Alte Pinakothek. Tintoretto devoted enormous energy to drawing, and there exist hundreds of examples of studies of particular aspects of movement. But he must have made very few drawings of complete compositions to judge by the fact that only two such examples are in existence. One is the preparatory drawing for this fine and unusual composition depicting a secular subject illustrated below. Vulcan's unexpected entry into the room of Venus has startled Mars into hiding under the furniture; Cupid looks on, smiling maliciously. The equilibrium of this composition indicates that it is a well thought-out work, marked more by elegance than by the artist's usual fury of creation. Pleasing features are the atmosphere of a Venetian palazzo, and the supple figures of Venus and Vulcan, the latter draped in striped Turkish silk. The orchestration of colour in the widely diffused light achieves a rare harmony due to the co-ordination of the sources of the light. On the basis of all these elements, the painting is to be dated just after 1550, when Tintoretto, within the framework of the manneristic structure introduced the methods of gradating light which he had learnt from Paolo Veronese. (Tietze suggests that the work is derived from *Mercury and Aeneas* by Daniele da Volterra.)

29-30 The Creation of the Animals, 1550-53. Oil on canvas, 157 × 270 cm. Venice, Accademia. Dated by Pittaluga (1925), this is one of five paintings executed for the Sala dell'Albergo of the Scuola della Trinità; the series had been begun by Torbido in 1547. It is a happy, decorative interpretation of the theme, a work of fantasy, where the artist seems to return to the didactic purpose of the mosaics of St Mark's and the powerful representations of animal forms found in Romanesque art: the birds in couples, the huge fish in the sea.

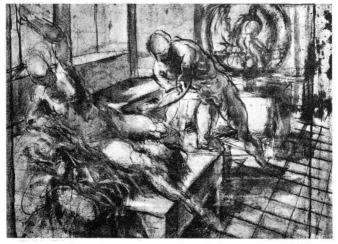

Study for 'Venus, Vulcan and Mars'. Berlin, Kupferstichkabinett

31-32 The Fall of Man, 1550-53. Oil on canvas, 145×208 cm. Venice, Accademia. For historical information, see notes to previous plate. The golden glow, the light which is imprisoned in colour, the enjoyment of landscape evoked by the rustling Garden of Eden, reveal the spirit of Titian as a fruitful source of inspiration, but not in the form of slavish imitation. It is Tintoretto who is responsible for the discreet range of colour tones and for the tortuous movement which is both formal and psychological.

33 St Louis of Toulouse with St George and the princess, 1552. Oil on canvas, 227×148 cm. Venice, Accademia. Dated by Pittaluga (1925), together with other works painted for the Camerlenghi salt directorate at the Rialto. The painting is characterized by its solid modelling and brilliant composition. The static and contemplative figure of the saint is balanced by the lively dialogue between St George and the princess. A happy idea is the placing of the princess astride the dragon, an image which was bound to strike the imagination of the common people. One can understand the indignation of Dolce, pedantically upholding the canons of 'decorum', but he would have been a better critic if he had noticed the refined treatment of the breast-plate of St George, in which is mirrored the vermilion robe worn by the princess.

34 Portrait of a Nobleman, 1553. Oil on canvas, 115×100 cm. Vienna, Kunsthistorisches Museum (No. 250). The portrait is inscribed with its date; this was the time when Tintoretto was most affected by the influence of Titian, which has been noted in the paintings for the Scuola della Trinità. This is an extremely refined and elegant example. The sitter may be a lawyer or a man of letters. His right hand rests on a book, but his gaze turns sadly elsewhere and escapes us. Two intertwined initials, and a certain physical resemblance, indicate that this may be a portrait of Lorenzo Soranzo, who appears in the large family portrait in the Museo del Castello, Milan.

35 Martyrdom of St Christopher, 1551-56. Oil on canvas, 425× 240 cm. Venice, Madonna dell'Orto. Together with *Four Angels bringing the Cross to St Peter*, this formed the wings of an organ case. The composition is very restrained, almost exceptionally so; the artist does not emphasize psychological and naturalistic details, but stresses the idea of the cruel and violent event which is taking place – as Newton has pointed out, no one could surpass Tintoretto in the creation of such *happenings*. St Christopher, the pivot around which the whole composition revolves, is seen against a background which is not void but filled with meaningful space and inundated with light.

36 The Presentation of the Virgin, 1556. Oil on canvas, 425× 448 cm. Venice, Madonna dell'Orto. Commissioned in 1551 and begun in 1556, the year when Tintoretto received the final payments.

The painting coincides with the period when the influence of Veronese became apparent in Tintoretto's search for a typological beauty, refinement of form and richness of decoration; for this reason it was particularly appreciated by Vasari. The construction of the perspective is perhaps rather theatrical, but strikes the imagination. Of particular interest is the graduated group of figures crowded together on the left: their contorted movements have been held to suggest some symbolic significance, but they may have been intended only as the poor and sick waiting at the threshold of the temple for alms.

37   St Ursula and her Virgins, c. 1555. Oil on canvas, 330×178 cm. Venice, San Lazzaro dei Mendicanti. From the church of the Incurabili. The probable date of execution is around 1555, when Tintoretto was painting under the influence of Veronese; this is suggested by the richness of its colour and the atmosphere of a fable, which recalls the biblical paintings in the Prado. The richly embroidered costumes and the stereotyped faces of the Virgins have caused some historians (notably Pallucchini, writing in 1950) to include this among the early works, but this is unlikely to be the case, owing to the masterly treatment of the spatial structure. The beauty of detail in this painting is such that the collaboration of assistants can be excluded (and hence also the possibility of its being a very late work). In the *Encyclopaedia of World Art*, 1967, Pallucchini gives the date 1554-5.

38-39   Moses bringing forth water from the rock, c. 1555. Oil on canvas, 118×180 cm. Frankfurt, Städelsches Kunstinstitut. This work has been variously dated: von Hadeln, writing in 1922, suggested 1560; Tietze gives 1544-7, and Pallucchini 1555. It is without doubt one of the works painted under the influence of Veronese, at the same time as the Prado ceilings and *St Ursula*. No hint is to be found in this work of the dramatic spirit which was to be expressed in the complex and agitated compositions of the San Rocco ceilings, painted in 1577.

40-41   Joseph and Potiphar's wife, c. 1555. Oil on canvas, 54×117 cm. Madrid, Prado. One of a series of Biblical studies: *Judith and Holofernes, The Chaste Susanna, The Finding of Moses, The Queen of Sheba before Solomon, Esther and Ahasuerus,* and *The Purification of the captured virgins of Midian* (repainted, so that it is considered a school painting by some historians, such as Berenson and Philips, while others, like Thode and Osmaston, date it to a later period). This group of paintings was according to Sánchez Cantón, bought by Velázquez for Philip IV of Spain, during his second stay in Venice. They are to be included among those painted when Tintoretto was strongly influenced by Veronese, around 1555, and, as can be seen from the perspective and rich decoration, they originally came from the ceiling of a Venetian palazzo. But this painting has more to offer than mere decoration: the ability to create a psychological situation and to exploit it fully by means of a pictorial language in which the lines of the composition are irregular and the range of colour elaborate and sumptuous. The nude body of Potiphar's wife, defined by a supple but not decorative line, shines with a brilliant light, contrasting with the dark red velvet of the alcove.

42-44 Susanna and the Elders, c. 1555. Oil on canvas, 146× 193 cm. Vienna, Kunsthistorisches Museum. This is without doubt one of the greatest masterpieces in the whole of sixteenth-century Venetian art. It marks the end of the period when Tintoretto's closeness to Veronese enabled him to try out combinations of clear and crystalline colours, delicate shadows and subtle reflections. In this beautiful evocation of nature there is a striking insistence on the colour green, in countless variations, and the sinuous form of Susanna stands out against this background as a weightless mass, defined by light. Newton has remarked that only Degas could capture such a gesture and create such an atmosphere of feminine intimacy. Yet it should be borne in mind that this beautiful image was created by Tintoretto out of his recollection of a classical Venus, such as the engravings of Raimondi had made known.

45 The Evangelists John and Mark, 1552-7. Oil on canvas, 257×150 cm. Venice, Santa Maria Zobenigo (or del Giglio). The outer doors of the organ loft depicted *The Conversion of St Paul*, now lost, which, in view of its subject matter and the other version of the same subject in the National Gallery, Washington, must have been lively and full of movement. With Tintoretto's usual love of contrast, the paintings for the inner doors are static portrayals of the solemn figures of the Evangelists with their symbols. They are arranged in pairs following a vertical perspective, upon clouds of a rock-like consistency. The figures are strikingly modelled in difficult postures against a livid background. Through the dense layers of dark colour it is possible to perceive the spiralling movement of the individual brushstrokes.

46 The Evangelists Luke and Matthew, 1552-57. Oil on canvas, 259×150 cm. Venice, Santa Maria Zobenigo (or del Giglio). See notes to previous plate.

47-50 Last Supper, c. 1560. Oil on canvas. 221×413 cm. Venice, San Trovaso. Painted for the Chapel of the Holy Sacrament, which was built in 1556. This is one of the most dramatic versions of this subject: Christ's revelation dismays his humble companions and imprints their gestures with an unexpected violence. The composition is based on an elliptical figure, of which Christ occupies the ideal and formal centre. The holy nature of the event is not lessened by the inclusion of naturalistic details, such as the coarse, rustic objects seen in the humble room, or by the portrayal of the apostles as ordinary men of the people.

51 Portrait of Alvise Cornaro, c. 1560-65. Oil on canvas, 112×
85 cm. Florence, Galleria Palatina, Pitti. Alvise Cornaro, the author
of *Vita Sobria* and humanistic treatises on architecture, died in 1566
at the age of ninety-one and, since in this portrait he appears to
be very old, it is reasonable to date it to between 1560 and 1565.
The style is of great refinement; it has been ascribed to Titian,
but the almost Rembrandtesque impression of light reduced to
luminous dust particles is clearly the creation of Tintoretto. The
portrait is also psychologically valid: from the extremely fragile
body – the bony structure can be seen under the surface of the
skin – there still emerges a forceful vitality of mind eagerly searching
for truth, though there is no trace of the eccentricity which is
apparent in the portrait of the same sitter by his friend Ruzzante.

52-53 The Discovery of the True Cross, 1561. Oil on canvas,
228×508 cm. Venice, Santa Maria Mater Domini. This work can
be dated fairly confidently to 1561, the year of the foundation of
the Scuola del Sacramento, for which it was painted. The composition
is particularly serene and elegant; the elongated female figures in
richly embroidered clothes are reminiscent of the portraits of
Parmigianino, and very close to the female figures in the *Adoration
of the Golden Calf* in the church of the Madonna dell'Orto (1560).
A lively contrast is created by the group of spectators on the left,
a series of humorous, naturalistic portraits.

54 The Removal of St Mark's Body, 1569. Oil on canvas,
422×516 cm. Venice, Accademia. In 1569, fourteen years after the
date of *St Mark rescuing a slave,* Dr Tommaso Rangone commissioned three other paintings for the series illustrating the life
of the great saint of Venice. We know from an existing engraving
by Zucchi (1720) that in the early nineteenth century the left-hand
side of this canvas was cut, and, in the centre, the pile of wood
prepared for the pyre was painted over; it was uncovered again when
the painting was cleaned in 1959, thus making sense of the
composition, and accounting for the storm which had been sent to
put out the fire and terrify the infidels. The dramatic effect is
enhanced by the placing of the focal group of figures in one corner,
against a ghostly architectural background.

55 The Finding of St Mark's Body, 1569. Oil on canvas,
405×405 cm, Milan, Brera. For historical notes, see previous plate.
The donor is again Dr Tommaso Rangone, who appears kneeling,
with outstretched arms. In the beautiful setting of this work a
receding vault, with regular repetition of columns and arches, creates
a sustained rhythm. The light plays over these architectural forms
and illuminates the ghost of St Mark, who points to the tomb in
which his body is hidden. At the same time, the saint works a
miracle, the healing of a paralytic. The boldly foreshortened figure
lying at the feet of the apparition is perhaps the corpse which is
to be substituted for the body of the saint. However, these subsidiary

episodes do not break up the unity of the composition, thanks to the rigorous and constructive handling of light.

56 Last Judgment, 1562. Oil on canvas. Venice, Madonna dell' Orto. Detail. Tintoretto executed this painting and its pendant, *The Adoration of the Golden Calf*, over a three-year period. Apart from the detail of Christ holding a sword and lily, which we find also in an engraving of Lucas van Leyden, Tintoretto's conception is truly original and grandiose. It is fairly obvious that the sense of a meteoric cataclysm, the roaring of turbulent waters, are the result of the artist's own attentive study of the Apocalypse, and not, as has been suggested, a combination of the themes of the Last Judgment and the Flood.

57-59 Crucifixion, 1564-65. Oil on canvas, 536×1224 cm. Venice, Scuola di San Rocco. Details. A year after entering into his contract with the directors of the Scuola di San Rocco, the artist began work on this great *Crucifixion*, completing it in 1565. It was greatly admired by his contemporaries and reproduced in engravings, among them one by Agostino Carracci in 1589. This work is an important milestone in Tintoretto's development, for in it light fulfils an expressive function, providing a unifying link between the separate, rounded groups of figures, distributed throughout the vast space.

60-61 Christ before Pilate, 1566-67. Oil on canvas, 522×405 cm. Venice, Scuola di San Rocco. This and the next two canvases completed the decoration of the Sala dell'Albergo which began with the Crucifixion (*pls 57-9*). From the first, the figure of Christ has been highly praised: 'Here is an action that is certainly divine; / What great draughtsmanship is in that figure! / He stands withdrawn in meditation / Wrapped all over in white linen / And appears naked'. (M. Boschini, *Carta del Navegar Pittoresco*, 1660). The diaphanous figure has a certain similarity with the figure of Christ in Pontormo's fresco in the Carthusian monastery at Galluzzo: perhaps the common origin is to be found in one of Dürer's engravings. Apart from the skilful use of the architectural background the painting is remarkable for the choral function of the tumultuous crowd – an effect obtained by the allusive method of showing lances, red banners and a small number of heads close together.

62-63 Ecce Homo, 1566-67. Oil on canvas, 285×400 cm. Venice, Scuola di san Rocco. See note to *pl. 60*. This painting is perhaps less famous than the others in the Sala dell'Albergo, but its unusual composition is very interesting. As in a classical tragedy, cruelty and horror remain behind the scenes and the spectator sees only their result: the bleeding figure of Christ abandoned on the steps, his atitude that of a resigned victim. The composition is very compressed, with the figures arranged so as to form a niche around Christ, while light fulfils the emotive function of focusing our attention on the martyred body and bloodstained shroud.

64 Christ bearing the Cross, 1566-67. Oil on canvas, 522×405 cm. Venice, Scuola di San Rocco. See note to *pl. 60*. The composition of the disjointed procession is most remarkable: in the lower part of the picture the procession moves forward in shadow, with the figures illuminated against a dark background, while in the upper section the figures stand out as dark forms against the green and blue tones of the sky, and the clouds bordered with light. It seems that Tintoretto is acting upon the advice of Mattia Bellintani to meditate on the sacrifice of Christ, 'look well on these things as if you were present . . . The Cross beats against the Crown of Thorns, which penetrate deeply'.

65 Philosopher, 1571-72. Oil on canvas, 234×137 cm. Venice, Libreria Sansoviniana. Painted in 1571-2 according to von Hadeln. Historians are divided as to the authorship of the whole group of *Philosophers*, but there is almost complete agreement that four or five at any rate are by the hand of Tintoretto and this is certainly a very fine example. The powerful body, painted in a manneristic rhythm, can scarcely be contained within the niche, and the shadow which spreads out to the left of the figure creates an illusion of a bodily presence.

66 Christ at the house of Martha and Mary, c. 1575. Oil on canvas, 197×131 cm. Munich, Alte Pinakothek. It is known that this canvas, which is signed, was formerly in the Dominican church of Augusta, for which it may have been painted. probably in about 1575. This might also explain the refinement and elegance of the treatment which could have been intended to meet the special requirements of a donor – a reasonable deduction when we consider some of the details attentively: the jewels worn by Mary, the shining copper and pewter vessels, the figure of the servant girl illuminated by the fire from the little stove. The structure of the group is particularly compressed in order to express the irresistible fascination Christ's words exert over Mary, and the colour, rich but not garish, is dominated by harmonies of blue and purple.

67-69 The Pool of Bethesda, 1559. Oil on panel, 238×560 cm. (Painted on the doors of the ambry.) Venice, Church of San Rocco. Documentary evidence dates this painting. When the cupboard was destroyed in the seventeenth century, the painting was altered in order to make it symmetrical with Fumiani's *Cleansing of the Temple*; it was restored to its present dimensions, an act of debatable wisdom, in 1937. The movement in the composition which causes the group of onlookers to bend down may have been taken from *St Mark rescuing a slave*, but here Tintoretto creates a constricted space, which conveys the impression of an excited crowd eagerly pushing forward. The new-found freedom of light gives an airy quality to the colour and dominates the formal structure. The figure of the sick man who has been cured and joyfully picks up his mattress is justly famous.

70-73 Nativity, 1576-81. Oil on canvas, 264×374 cm. Venice, Scuola di San Rocco. Details. This is the first of the paintings for the outer wall of the upper hal¹. The first thing which strikes the viewer is the originality of the artist's invention – the rustic hay-loft with patches of light entering through the beams and falling upon the figures which are arranged in two different planes. The structure of the composition is taken from an engraving in Dürer's *Little Passion*, but it is infused by Tintoretto's warmth of feeling and skilful colour orchestration. In the upper section there is a calm and solemn atmosphere, while below the adoring shepherds turn and twist about in joyful motion. creating a musical counterpoint.

74-75 Baptism of Christ, 1576-81. Oil on canvas, 538×465 cm. Venice, Scuola di San Rocco. This painting is placed beside the *Nativity*, but the spatial treatment of the two works is entirely different: here Tintoretto avoids all centrality or parallelism, and allows the viewer a glimpse of the partly hidden figure undressing on the right and of the lay brother, who adds a curious note to the picture. The principal figures, Christ and St John, are placed on the middle plane, by a river bank whose gentle curve is indicated by the shape of the long line of people awaiting baptism and by the deeply bowed head of Christ. The threatening clouds may be intended as symbols of the tragedy which was to end the life of the Messiah whom John is revealing to the multitude.

76-77 Bacchus, Ariadne and Venus, 1578. Oil on canvas, 146× 167 cm. Venice, Doge's Palace. Together with three others, *Minerva driving back Mars, The Three Graces,* and *Vulcan and the Cyclopes,* this painting was placed in the Sala dell'Anticollegio in 1716 on being transferred from the Salotto Dorato, for which it had originally been painted. They form a series of allegories of the birth of Venice and the virtues of her government. The secular subject and the decorative purpose of the paintings led the great visionary to select the elements in his art which were best adapted to such elegant fables: extremely flexible rhythms, a softened chiaroscuro, luminous colour, beauty of the female form. *Bacchus, Ariadne and Venus*, perhaps the most beautiful of the four paintings, represents the birth of Venice on the seashore, enriched by divine grace and crowned with liberty.

78-79 The Three Graces, 1578. Oil on canvas, 146×167 cm. Venice. Doge's Palace. For general notes, see previous plate. In this composition, also, harmony of line heightens and reinforces the soft, plastic forms of the figures with a repeated rhythm and a succession of parallel cadences. The figures are portrayed in the open air, beneath a tree whose leaves seem to be swaying in the wind and creating areas of light and shade on the smooth flesh; even in so formal a composition, the force of the artist's emotion enables him to give permanence to a passing moment of reality.

80-81   The Temptation of St Anthony, c. 1577. Oil on canvas, 282×165 cm. Venice, San Trovaso. This is thought to have been painted at the same time as the allegorical works in the Doge's Palace, that is in about 1577, and it may have been commissioned by Antonio Milledonne, Secretary to the Senate. However, in this painting the somewhat academic polish of the allegories is avoided. This is due to the exceptional dynamism of the composition, which, with its confusion of intertwined limbs, is nevertheless balanced, and to the harmony between colour and light, which unite in defining the modelled forms. The beautiful, half-naked female figures did not prevent this picture from being placed in a Venetian church, even at a time when the Counter-Reformation was in full swing elsewhere.

82   The Rape of Helen (Naval Battle), c. 1580. Oil on canvas, 186×137 cm. Madrid, Prado. Detail. This was one of the paintings bought by Velázquez for Philip IV and is not the same as the version executed by Tintoretto in 1562 for Cardinal Ercole Gonzaga, being obviously a later work. It is similar in style to the paintings of the *Glorious Deeds of the Gonzaga Family*, as well as to some of those in the Lower Hall of the Scuola di San Rocco, all painted around 1580. There is a similar contrast between the modelled groups of figures in the foreground and the moving crowds, suggested by rays of light. In all the Gonzaga paintings the work of assistants is apparent, but in this picture it seems that Tintoretto was responsible for most of the work, and especially for the clarity of effects of light.

83-84   Paradise, c. 1579. Oil on canvas, 143×362 cm. Paris, Louvre. Thought to be a *modello* – a detailed preliminary painting – for the competition announced in 1579 for the redecoration of the Great Council Chamber (other artists who competed included Veronese, Francesco Bassano and Palma Giovane). According to Ridolfi, this painting was in the collection of the Counts Bevilacqua of Verona. Not only Domenico but also the whole of Tintoretto's studio contributed to the execution of this vast composition. It is possible, also, that certain changes were requested by the authorities; whatever the reason, the final work has lost that unity of composition which distinguishes this *modello*.

85-86   Flight into Egypt, 1583-87. Oil on canvas, 422×580 cm. Venice, Scuola di San Rocco. Part of the last group of paintings executed for the Lower Hall of the Scuola di San Rocco between 1583 and 1587. Tintoretto interpreted this subject in a modern sense, with the landscape seen as a projection of the emotions of the protagonists. Here again it seems that Bellintani's guide to religious contemplation (1573) may have proved valuable to Tintoretto: ' You will set off on the journey with Mary and Joseph, most diligently contemplating their method of travelling '; the illusion of continuous and wearisome movement is expressed in their submissive bodies. The monk also describes the fatigues and dangers of the journey, arising both from things and from men; and this is the reason for their advance along a hidden path, where they are protected by the greenery. The colour is rather vibrant in tone, especially in the focal group of figures, and harmonizes with the luminous sunset in the vast sky where the ranks of clouds seem to climb immeasurable heights.

87-90 Last Supper, 1593-94. Oil on canvas, 365×568 cm. Venice, San Giorgio Maggiore. This work, together with its pendant, *The Gathering of Manna*, can be dated on the basis of records of payments. Although this is largely a studio painting, it was without doubt Tintoretto himself who conceived the idea for the two large canvases, so diverse and contrasting in tone. *The Last Supper* is especially moving; it was painted only a few months before Tintoretto's death and contains a high degree of fantasy. In this work the artist returns to the composition of the San Rocco version of the same subject but handles it with a greater depth of emotion; the vast space is illuminated by the light of a smoking torch, making the shadows dense and peopling them with dematerialized angelic forms. To justify the contrasting, and thematically extraneous, figures in the foreground of this composition Tintoretto might have echoed what Veronese said of his own *Last Supper*, ' if there is surplus space in the picture, then I adorn it with figures according to my invention'; they have nevertheless been subordinated to the visionary solemnity of the holy scene.

1

2

3

4

5

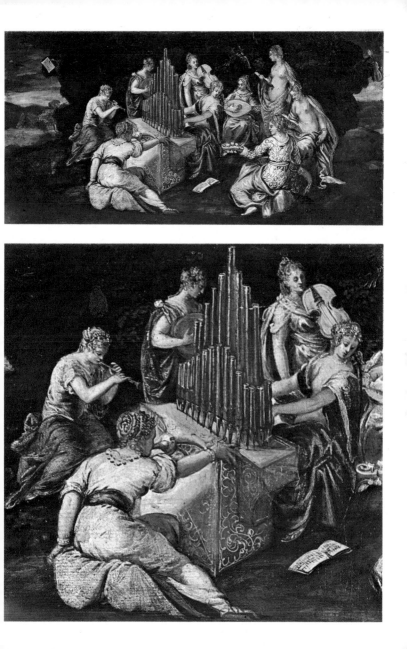

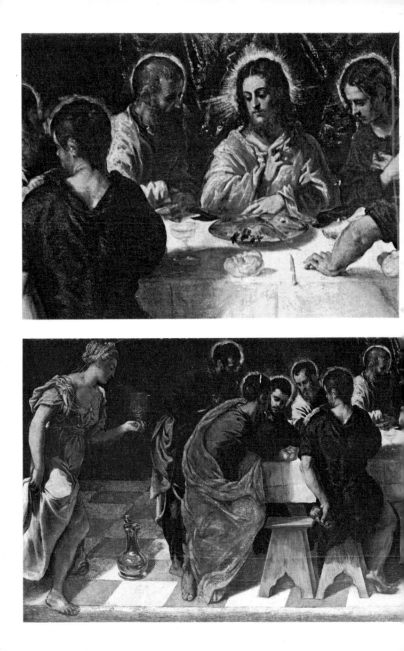

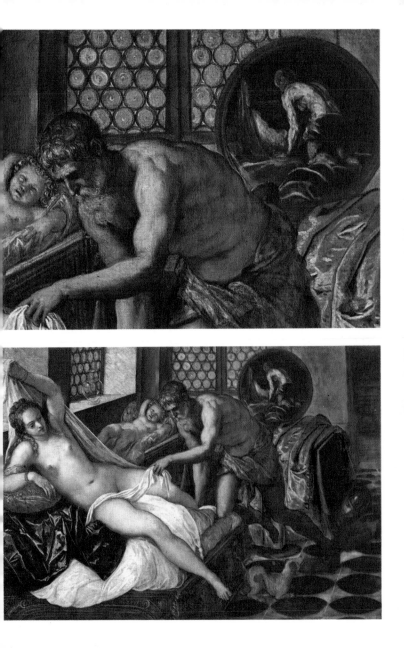

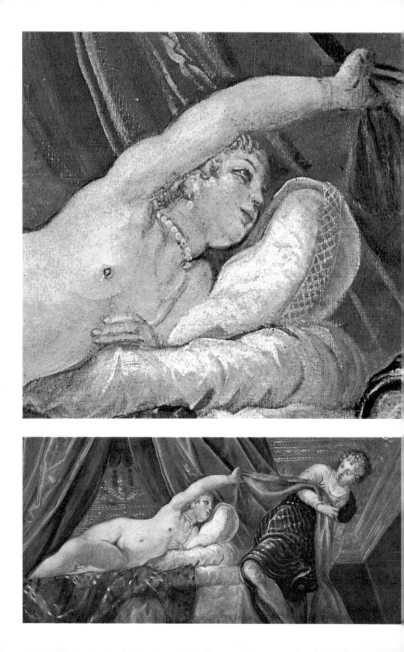

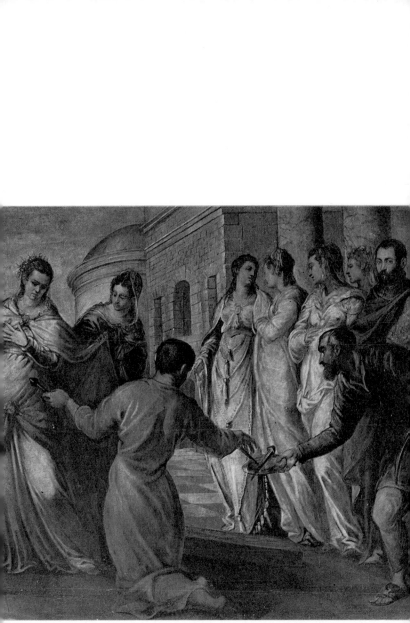

3

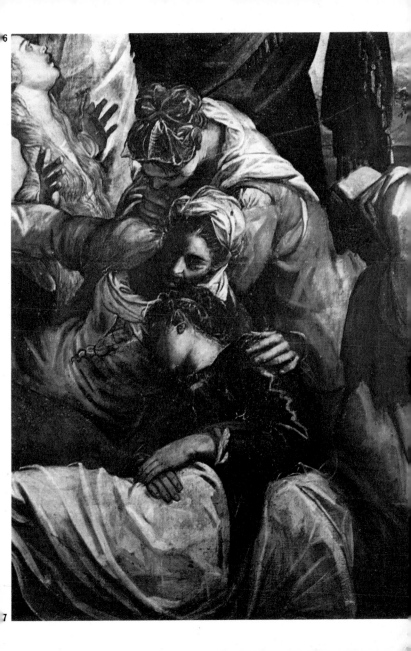